Spirit† Writ††en Life

Emily Zondlak

Chapbook Press

Schuler Books
2660 28th Street SE
Grand Rapids, MI 49512
(616) 942-7330
www.schulerbooks.com

Spirit Written Life

ISBN 13: 9781948237574

eBook ISBN: 9781948237581

Library of Congress Control Number: 2020915506
(Paperback edition)

Copyright © 2020 Emily Zondlak

All rights reserved. No part of this book may be reproduced in any form except for the purpose of brief reviews, without written permission of the author.

Printed in the United States by Chapbook Press.

A thank you to Mrs. Paige Herrema for capturing phenomenal pictures illuminating my old self to become a new creation in Jesus Christ's image and for God's glory!

Spirit†Writ††en Life

Many people describe me; once they look pass my disability, as happy-go-lucky, always smiling, and someone who has a great-sense-of-humor. Often, some may say that the joy of the Lord and Jesus' light shines brightly from me! I was not always joyful or a beaming light for Jesus Christ. God has been writing and planning my life's journey, leading and guiding me to Him to have an intimate relationship with Him even before He created me in my mom's womb. This is how God transformed a spirit written life into my testimony.

I was born with a physical disability called Cerebral Palsy. Also, I am nonverbal, which means that my speech is difficult to understand. Having Cerebral Palsy does not shorten my years on earth. When God calls me home in Heaven to be with Him and Jesus, is when my time on this old earth will end and my purpose will be complete.

Upon my grand entrance in this world, my mom was not feeling well and just had a blah feeling all day. While my dad was working, he called my mom to check to see how she was doing. Several times he told my mom to call the doctor to explain how she was feeling. My mom did not call the doctor - all that she wanted to do was sleep. She had not gone into labor or experienced contractions before because my sisters were born five-weeks premature with a C-Section. So she was experiencing contractions with me and did not realize it.

That night she, my dad, and sisters went to bed early for the night. In the middle of the night, my mom thought that the waterbed had sprung a leak so she woke my dad up and headed toward the bathroom. Noticing that the supposed leak was trailing behind her, my mom realized that her water had broken so my dad called the doctor. The doctor asked what color the fluid was; it was clear. So off to the hospital the three of us went as advised by the doctor. Nurses and doctors greeted my mom by the Emergency entrance of the hospital because my parents' primary doctor called ahead of time to prepare them. While my dad was trying to find a parking spot to park the car and by the time my dad got to her room, my mom was hooked up to many monitors. The waiting game and visiting with family had begun.

Many hours later, my mom experienced extremely severe pain as if a sharp knife was jabbing her in her uterus. Her uterus ruptured and the doctors had to perform an emergency C-Section. My mom's and my life were in danger and the doctors did not know if either one of us would live. I was whisked away to the extremely highest Intensive Care Unit, in which I was hooked to many monitors. Wires and patches covered my frail body, and a nurse was one-on-one with me for assistance.

My parents had not seen me because they were concerned about my mom's health and wellbeing. My dad says that he did not officially meet me until four days after I was born because my parents wanted to see me together. My parents do not remember the time frame, in which I was relocated from the extremely highest Intensive Care Unit to just the Intensive Care Unit; where I was just hooked up to monitors. They could not hold me so they just placed their hands on my body whenever they came to see me. After three weeks of staying in the hospital; my parents switching off days and nights to attend to me while also taking care of my sisters and other responsibilities, they could take me home.

Once advised on how to gavage feed me, and an informational discussion on my birth happenings, my parents took me home. Gavage feeding is a tube placed through my nose that carried formula to my stomach so that I could eat.

When I went in for my four-month checkup, the doctor diagnosed me as having Cerebral Palsy because I smiled more than a normal baby and could not hold my head up on my own. During my birth, the lack of oxygen for the three to seven minutes, my brain was not receiving was what caused me to have Cerebral Palsy. My parents had not heard of Cerebral Palsy and so they researched it. Cerebral Palsy has a broad spectrum of how minimal or severe the disabilities will be for someone who has been diagnosed with this physical disability. It effects the movement of the body. It reduces the range of motion of the body, such as stiffness of the joints and effects swallowing. Cerebral Palsy causes impaired movement associated with abnormal reflexes. Some people who have Cerebral Palsy may be able to walk, while others cannot walk. It depends on the severity of Cerebral Palsy.

With me being diagnosed with this disability, the journey began of seeing doctors, therapists, running tests, and having occupational therapy. My parents and I traveled to some of the Midwest states to see if my diagnosis of Cerebral Palsy was correct. Some doctors gave me shots other than the normal immunization shots and I do not know the reasons behind these shots. On one occasion, my mom remembers, a doctor gave me a shot that caused my body to become limp like a noodle. I was very sleepy. Traveling and visiting doctors, therapists, and having occupational therapy was a new world for my parents. They raised me in the best way they knew without having huge differences from the way they were raising my sisters.

I began to learn how to live in my physical disabled body with all the help of my doctors and therapists. They instructed my parents on the best ways of helping my body. I had and still have specialized equipment to make things easier. I can walk, but I need assistance, which means someone needs to wrap his or her arms around my body as if he or she were a seatbelt or a safety harness. I have to be the person who is leading to the place where I want to go. My pace is slow so it takes time for me to go anywhere.

Before I was in school, I had different chairs that helped strengthen the core of my body. I had a stander equipment that was designed with a focus on positioning, modularity and growth. I stood in a spot for a certain period of time with a safety harness around my body to strengthen my legs.

When I was in school, I had walkers that had four wheels on them. In gym class, I was put in my walker for exercise; walking and running around trying to be like the other kids. I had to have AFO's, which are braces for my feet to correct my feet to be straight and to avoid my ankles from rolling as I walk. As I grew, I had to get new AFO's and they were not fun to make. I had to make my jerky body sit still for the doctor to make a cast-like shell of my feet. Once it hardens and the doctor is finished forming it with his hands, he has to cut the casts off. This process is not fun and the doctor has to do it twice for each foot. Once the casts were formed, I had to wait for a few weeks in order for them to be made into hard plastic. AFO's are not comfortable when they were made back in my day. I think today they have improved them. God blessed me with understanding parents who allowed me to wear my AFO's only when I exercised. I had different walkers that helped me walk to strengthen my legs.

During my school career, I had occupational therapy to help strengthen my body or loosen my muscles. I did not like being treated as I quote, "a textbook about Cerebral Palsy." At times, I did not feel as if I was being treated as a human being. Therapists advised with instructions on what I should and should not do. I acted as if I was going to do what they said, but once they were gone, I did not obey. I learned real fast on how to act around doctors and therapists.

I was taken out of class in which the students were learning the basics, to have occupational therapy, which meant having to work on my posture, kneeling, balancing, throwing and catching objects as well as getting in and out of my wheelchair safely. Occupational therapy was like a game that my therapists would try to create so that I would exercise and yet have fun.

Mary Free Bed Rehabilitation Hospital is a care inpatient rehabilitation hospital for children and adults who have experienced injuries related to the brain and spinal cord. They help people who have strokes, amputees, or illnesses requiring physical rehabilitation. I have been going to Mary Free Bed as long as I can remember. Parking in the covered parking lot and driving my wheelchair through the halls of Mary Free Bed in the nineteen-nineties and early years of two thousands, the décor was not bright and colorful as it is today. The walls were blah and the only brightness and fun part it had was the skywalk. The skywalk had huge windows that viewed a lot of the city of Grand Rapids, Michigan and I liked it because of the solar lighting. It had a ramp built into the floor so when I drove my wheelchair through the skywalk, I felt as though I was riding a mini roller coaster.

At Mary Free Bed, the doctors and therapists saw that my speech was not audible for anyone to understand me. So my life consisted of not only completing exercises to strengthen my upper and lower body, but now speech therapy was added to the mix besides going to Mary Free Bed for wheelchairs. God blessed me with determination and so if an exercise was challenging, by golly, I completed the task no matter how long it took. My parents' mentality was "Do not say she can't. Let her try and do the task in her own way."

In the years of nineteen-nineties and early two thousands, technology was not instant and compacted like it is today. Therapists worked on developing and improving my skills by having me say words or point to objects then say the name on flashcards.

When I started school, I had a speech device called DynaVox, which was a portable speech-generating device that resembles a tablet PC. It was a popular augmentative and alternative communication device designed to enable people who cannot speak to access the words needed to create messages and converse. I had to remember sequences to make a sentence and my DynaVox had overlays that had different images on them to create more sentences to help me communicate. Another communication device that I had in the early years of two thousands was called Vanguard. It was a full-sized, dynamic display communication device featuring synthesized and digitized speech. It helped with exploring targeting, picture recognition, associations and vocabulary options. It was electronic and I had to remember button sequences to create sentences. My Vanguard had the basic little kid songs and two games on it.

I have a gag reflex so my parents and I learned which foods I can and cannot eat or how to add stuff to the food so that I can eat it. My food has to be soft. Much like a toddler has his or her food prepared, my food has to be cut up in little pieces. I also drink with a straw. Someone has to feed me because I do not have the dexterity to feed myself. I cough every few bites and with liquids as well. My coughing is my normal routine when eating or drinking.

My dad was raised to be Catholic so essentially, I was raised Catholic. I believed that I was going to Heaven because I sort of believed in God, participated in communion and performed all of the traditional practices. My parents decided to baptize me when I was a baby.

Catholics celebrate communion at every service, but a person has to be seven or eight years old before he or she can consume Jesus Christ's body and blood for the first time. I attended the handicapped catechism classes, in which I learned about Jesus, how to pray the "Our Father" and the "Hail Mary" prayers. I also learned the Rosary, which is a form of prayer used especially in the Catholic Church named for the string of knots or beads used to count the component prayers. With the Rosary, the prayers prayed are the *Apostles' Creed*, the *Our Father*, three *Hail Marys*, the *Glory Be*, the *Hail Holy Queen*, and the believer repeats these prayers seven times or so before the Rosary is completed. Baby baptism, first communion, confirmation, and confession are sacraments. Each sacrament is an outward sign of an inward grace.

I knew all the Catholic liturgy, in which, I said things when really I did not know what to say. I was the kind of believer who repeated the same prayer continuously to where I was not thinking about what I was praying. It was routine, but when troubled circumstances arose, I was constantly in prayer. I felt I was a Pharisee because they believed that they received a check mark or a pat on the back for praying prayers. Pharisees rely on traditions that do not come from the heart; these traditions or sacraments make a person look holy. God wants mercy not sacrifice. He examines the heart, not outer appearances.

Communion is celebrated at service or mass, which is the way Catholics refer to it. Believers consume bread and wine, which symbolizes Jesus Christ's body and blood shed on the cross because of His great love for His children. Communion is a remembrance of the Last Supper, in which Jesus told His disciples that one of them was going to betray Him because He was going to be crucified on the cross. Before Jesus was crucified on the cross, He prayed earnestly; wept bitterly that His sweat was like blood falling on the ground. Jesus was betrayed by one of His disciples with a kiss. This disciple handed Him over to be arrested because the world did not and continues to not believe in Jesus Christ or God the Father. Jesus' disciples abandoned Him and denied knowing Him. Jesus stood before the guards and they mocked Him. The guards made a crown of thorns and put it on Jesus' head, which pierced His skull. Jesus' garments were torn off from Him and were sold. The guards beat Jesus with chained whips that tore His body - it has been said that after Jesus was beaten no one recognized Him. That is how brutally Jesus was beaten! Jesus was questioned and falsely accused. The time came when Jesus was crucified on the cross and because of how brutally Jesus was beaten, Simon, a local person helped Jesus carry the cross to Golgotha. The guards whipped them along the way. At Golgotha, the guards stripped off Jesus' linen garments. With harsh treatment, nails pierced Jesus' hands and feet because He was hanged on the cross. Jesus was mocked again and insults were hurled at Him. Darkness plunged the earth. Luke 23:45-46 says, "And the curtain of the temple was torn in two. Jesus called out with a loud voice, "Father, into your hands I commit my spirit." When he had said this, he breathed his last." Jesus went down to Hades and conquered death by death because He rose from the grave and is seated at the right-hand-side of God! Communion is declaring that one day very soon Jesus is coming back, but there will be a new Heaven and a new earth. God, Jesus, and Holy Spirit will be fellowshipping with His children.

When I was immature in my faith, I remember telling my friend that I was going to

Heaven because I participated in communion. I did not know what I was talking about and was probably tired of listening to her praising God. I was defending my faith because Catholics have all the answers and other denominations do not or so I thought.

Catholics have a tradition called Confession, where it is practiced before the major holidays of Easter and Christmas. Confession is where a believer can go into a room behind a curtain and confess his or her sins before the priest. Then the priest will pray to God about the sins that were confessed. Then live life his or her way! I completed the traditions of the Catholic faith, but doing them, I felt as though I was just going through the motions. I did not have an intimate relationship with God. I just knew of Him. I wanted to make my parents proud of me when I completed each sacrament and I was following their lead.

School was important to me and I started at an earlier age than most children do. The community where I was being raised offered to take me to my school even though I was not apart of their school district. My parents were concerned, but my dad said that I was excited to attend school. Remember, I am disabled and was in a manual wheelchair so I would have been concerned, too, if I were in my parents' shoes. My mom was worried about me on my first day of school. She called the school and said that she was coming to pick me up. The staff reassured her that I was fine and was having fun. All that I remember from that school was playing, listening to music, and attending speech therapy.

    I transitioned from that special needs intermediate school to a public school district when I was five years old. I was the first handicapped student to attend that elementary. God blessed me with two God-loving women who were my aides. One was with me from Kindergarten to part of fifth grade and my other aide was from the last part of fifth grade to twelfth grade. I was mainstreamed through my school career, which means I was in classes with my age group of classmates, but had some help in different areas, such as reading, writing and math. As I passed my mainstream classes, teachers put me in general education classes. At the end of each school year, my parents attended a meeting with teachers and therapists to discuss what the plan was for the next school year. My parents were hesitant about me moving onto the next grade. My mom wanted them to hold me back and asked if they were passing me along just because of my disability. They advised her that they were not and encouraged my parents that I was ready to move onto the next grade.

    My two aides and staff members became my friends because people who are my age are usually not too willing to be my friend. Some cannot look past my disability and challenges. God put my aides, teachers, and staff members into my life to help me sort of look deeper to Him. When they shared their beliefs about Christ, I always listened

to avoid being rude. Friends would give me
Christian CDs for different reasons and I would like
them, but was not thinking about God in the songs.

School was part of my social life. My family
and staff members would comment about my smile
and my happy-go-lucky attitude as well as my
great-sense-of-humor. In my elementary school
years, I kept my feelings to myself. I did not want
my parents, sisters or staff members to fight my
battles because I wanted to fight them. During
recesses, some students would tease me and I would
talk back to them, but they would begin to tease me
about my speech. I did not take my communication
device everywhere that I went.

God has blessed me with the gift of
patience. Figuring out what I am trying to
communicate to you can be tricky. My family has to
figure out what I am trying to say also. People
should not feel bad when they do not understand my
speech off the bat. When trying to figure out what I
am communicating, have me repeat myself many

times. Also you can say, "Spell it." The tricky part is figuring out what letters I am saying, and remembering, and putting the letters together of what I spelled. Another way to communicate with me is by asking "Yes or No" questions and allowing me to answer. I like to use my natural voice box even though it is difficult for me to express my thoughts.

Sometimes I rode around through the schoolyard thinking: *Why can't I be like the regular kids who have friends?* I have many fake friends in my life. My definition of fake friends is to have someone talk to you and feel as if he or she cares about you one day, and the next he or she does not speak to you. That person ignores you.

I was not content with my disability and did not like that it was noticeable. Something inside of me kept encouraging me to be determined. I had to prove to teachers and students that I was smart. I had to put extra effort into my school assignments than other students; it took me triple the time to use my computer and specialized devices in order to complete assignments. Even though I smiled, had a happy-go-lucky attitude and a great-sense-of-humor, I was not joyful or content. I would wake up and would wish that it would be nighttime. I just lived life day-by-day because I had no hope.

Often when I drool uncontrollably or when I am eating in public, many people are grossed out or appalled by my messy routines. Instances in which they are uncomfortable speaking to me, they will either ignore me or speak to me as if I am a toddler. I become immune in having conversations because I become tired of the stereotypical behaviors. Having people not understand me or do not know what to say is difficult to deal with, but with patience, I can be understood.

I participated in downhill skiing with my family, Little League T-Ball, and hip-hop dance classes to be active. Seasons in my life through these activities, I was just trying to fill a need to be accepted for the person I was. Of course, these activities did not erase that empty feeling in my heart. I was trying to live up to the worldviews of being satisfied. I would watch age appropriate TV shows, movies, and I enjoyed listening to soft rock and country music. In my teenage years, I watched criminal TV shows as well as chick-flick and romance movies.

I participated in other adult friends' youth groups while my Catholic church offered a disability class, but I was too far advanced than the other students and that class became boring. Every year we would learn the same things as we did the year before. My aide invited me to her church youth group called Gems and I attended that up until the cut-off age. I liked the activities that I was involved in, but I did not choose to commit my life fully to God. My aide invited my mom and I to different seasonal programs at her church, and we would always attend to support her. I went to another disability high school aged youth group when my teacher invited me, but I was too educated to have fun at that one. I bounced around from youth group to youth group from middle school to high school. I was attending these different youth groups for the wrong reason. I was attending in hopes of having friends instead of establishing a relationship with God. I was trying to fill an empty space in my heart with friends my age.

The opportunity to attend Young Life Camp arose, and that was the second time I was away from my parents. While attending the Young Life Camp, I listened to everything that was taught through the week. I was half listening and understanding. At the beginning of each message, everyone sang along to praise and worship songs. I saw students lifting their hands and dancing. They seemed as though they were having a blast, but I was under a dark cloud not having as much fun as they were having. I was just going through the motions of life; putting a smile on my face, being outgoing, and having a great attitude. From the messages I understood that I had to open up the door of my heart for Jesus to come into my life. It was my choice whether or not to look at life as half-full or half-empty. The camp had set times for everyone to pray. I contemplated about my life and was angry with God for making me disabled instead of praying. I thought that God made me to have Cerebral Palsy and to be nonverbal for 20 years. As God matured my faith in Him, I realized that the birthing process caused this. Arriving home from Young Life Camp, I told my loved ones all about what I did at camp, such as, I went zip lining, tubing, completed a ropes course, went biking even though I did not pedal at all, danced at the dances, and went rock climbing. I also shared with my loved ones that the food was OK and the people who fed me. I put an imaginary mask on and pretended as if I drew nearer to Jesus when really, I did not. God's seed was scattered and watered inside of me, but no fruit surfaced. I lived in the darkness, in which I had no hope, joy, or peace. I acted as if I did not know what this person was talking about, but I did know. This addiction lasted until my teenage years when God opened my eyes to see this was an idol. Breaking this addiction was not easy, but with God's help, it was accomplished.

God is a jealous God. He does not want idols in my life because He wants my entire being to be completely surrendered to Him. I had to let God help me die to myself. This means not doing the things the world says is acceptable, such as watching cruel movies that have many intimate scenes, using swear words and drugs. Instead doing activities that I learned and know that they are pleasing to God, such as listening to praise songs, helping others, and watching movies that glorify God. It is a gradual process.

Many people treat handicapped people differently. They are not sure how to handle or act around the disabled so they often wear their kid gloves. Their voices become high-pitched and squeaky. Also their tone can come to be the other extreme, in which it is calm, understanding, and will give encouragements out excessively. People speak around me as if I am not present and cannot understand what they are speaking about. Of course, in school, students stared at me and had conversations around me too. I felt as though I stuck out like a sore thumb. I was drowning in hopelessness, but I was determined to prove everyone wrong by earning my diploma and attending school dances.

In my high school career, my best friend invited me to come to her youth group at Resurrection Life Church and I declined the invite. I made my homework an excuse of not attending. A few times, different friends invited me to their youth groups and my homework was always my excuse because it took me longer to complete homework than non-disabled students.

In the 10th grade, my best friend who was my age moved to Arizona for three years to take care of her grandmother. I felt lost without her because she looked past my disability. We bonded since the seventh grade. She and I e-mailed each other almost every day so I went to her for everything. My aide and her started a Bible Study over the phone because she experienced something terrible in her life. They invited me to join, but I gave them my homework excuse, of course, and did not join.

A characteristic of mine is that I always have been determined to live life to the fullest and not let my disability hold me back. During my high school career, I attended the Homecoming dances, Prom, and played in the Powder Puff game. In my junior year, I had my first boyfriend. At that time I did not know what love really was. The worldviews are totally and completely the opposite of God's love, what true love really is!

My senior year of high school was not my best year. I was not with my aide by her side as I was since the fifth grade. Teachers wanted to separate us to give me more independence. Well, having a friend be ripped from arms length was very depressing. She was someone who I shared life's moments with, my family, my strengths and weaknesses, and my likes as well as my dislikes. She loved me as if she was my mother. We hung out socially. Our relationship went beyond school and was a closely knitted friendship.

All of my senior year I acted as if I was happy and everything was fine. I think I was functionally depressed because I did not want to get out of bed. I forced myself to smile and laugh. In reality, I was mourning the loss of being by my aide's side all school day because we talked as friends did; laughed silly. I put on my happy-go-lucky attitude, smile, and great-sense-of-humor masks trying to be cooperative of being independent and going to classes alone and taking full responsibility of my schoolwork; e-mailing teachers asking for notes. I felt as though I was drowning. I pushed myself to earn good grades because I thought everyone assumed that I earned good grades because of my aide. Once again, I had to prove that I was smart. I was angry and depressed; I did not want to attend school. I did not share my feelings; I rolled with the flow.

A friend invited me to her youth group at Resurrection Life Church in the morning. I could not use my homework excuse so I told her I would have to ask my parents, and also see if I had homework that night. I had mixed emotions about wanting to attend. I bet my friend saw that I was worn out and suffocating by carrying my burdens around.

That night I had a little bit of homework to complete. So I asked my parents if I could go to this youth group, and they said, "Yes." and drove me there. I enjoyed it very much and attended there whenever I did not have homework. Listening and singing to praise songs about God, I related them to people in my life who I loved instead of God. The praise band sang songs glorifying God, Jesus, and Holy Spirit. I sang, but mostly, I lip sang because I was afraid of my speech being mocked. People were friendly, but often they engaged in conversations around me with their friends instead of speaking to me. People acted in the two types of stereotypes that I was used to; the high-pitched and squeaky tone of voice approach. Or the other tone of voice approach was calm, understanding, and gave encouragements out excessively.

When my senior year of high school had ended, my parents wanted me in some sort of activity during the summer so I would not be bored. One morning, God planned for my mom and I to attend a Resurrection Life Church service. While driving back home, I was looking through the bulletin for an activity to do. Holy Spirit led me to a group called Access, and it sounded interesting. I joined for all of the wrong reasons. It was something I could attend during the summer and was in my age group of people. The first few months I was about having friends because I had the world's mindset. I typed up a little blurb about my hopes, interests, and how my university online worked. When someone started speaking to me and could not understand me, I handed him or her this blurb. Attending this youth group and hearing that when God is in your life, you will be changed. You will live life differently. I often thought it would not be true and that this was crazy. I watched criminal TV shows, watched chick-flick and romance movies, and enjoyed listening to country music. So I thought that I would not change my interests, hobbies, or anything else for that matter. I wanted to be accepted for the person I was, past my disability. I had dreams of dating, getting married, and having adventures with friends.

There were times when I felt alone and as if I could not move forward anymore; God carried me while He strengthen our relationship and He used the youth group called Access for me to realize that I needed Jesus Christ to be my Lord and Savior.

There were times when I felt as if college was getting in the way of life especially when I had to spend seven days a week on schoolwork. There were times when God reminded me to reach for Him, to hold onto His hand, and to feel His embrace around me when I needed comfort or reassurance. God opened my eyes of my heart to realize that He has been with me on my life's journey.

In October of 2009 I surrendered my life fully to Lord Jesus Christ, my Savior and my God. I confessed with my mouth and believed in my heart that Jesus Christ is Lord; I was saved and became apart of God's family and His kingdom! I hit my rock bottom and God became real. God was not distant and I did not have to complete rituals or sacraments for God to love me. Religion kills the soul, but relationship with the Holy Spirit brings life when I am intimate with God; speaking to Him about my daily life. I said "Goodbye" to religion and going through the motions in my parents' church as well as friends' faith. I was being a pew warmer believer.

When I believed in my heart that Jesus Christ is Lord and decided to have an intimate relationship with God, I cried. My burdens Jesus lifted off from me. I felt as though God breathed His breath of life in me. He flipped His light in me so darkness fled from me. God's rivers of living water were as though I was driving my wheelchair on them as I moved. My fears were gone. I felt as though Jesus' light was beaming in me; smiling from ear-to-ear. I had unspeakable joy!

God put the desire in my heart to be baptized and He planned it to make it public on January 29, 2012. How I want to live is my choice. I can live in the party scene and think that it is what satisfies. When I made the decision to surrender my life to Jesus Christ as my personal Lord and Savior and was baptized, I have been set free from bondage. I have the incredible gift, blessing, and privilege from Lord God Almighty to believe, trust, and obey God my Father.

Baptism meant to declare that I was finished following the authority of sin, Internet sex and other addictions. I was deciding to obey God Almighty, Jesus Christ, and Holy Spirit in life. I was deciding to love, forgive, pray, and lend a helping hand in life.

Several years later, God matured my faith in Him, He told me that I needed His wonderful gift of Holy Spirit to be led and guided in life. I thought I had His Holy Spirit living inside of me because I decided to surrender my life to Jesus and was baptized. I had to asked Father God for His promised gift of Holy Spirit.

God guided me to attend a small church, in which taught sound doctrine. We, the Church, are a local gathering of followers of Jesus Christ. We believe in the New Testament Church, the validity of the Bible, the present ministry of the Holy Spirit in and through believers, and the need to assemble together. We believe that only through accurate study of God's Word are we able to fully know and understand God's will for our lives. So a year of studying the Bible while attending Sunday morning church services and weekly Bible Study, God planned for me to attend a Bible Study to understand better His Holy Spirit in-depth. John Bevere with Addison Bevere have a book entitled *The Holy Spirit: An Introduction Book* in which, they explain God's Holy Spirit.

It was the second to the last Bible Study session and I wanted God's awesome gift of the Holy Spirit to be living and dwelling within me. November of 2015, I asked my Bible Study to pray for me. They huddled around me, prayed to God to bless me with His Holy Spirit. Some of them laid their hands on me while praying, speaking in tongues to God.

The incredible gift of speaking in tongues is another way to pray to God; praying God's perfect will, and encouraging yourself. The Holy Spirit will give you God Almighty's wisdom, understanding, and discernment. The Holy Spirit is in you (if you ask Father God for this gift) by leading, guiding, teaching, and reminding you the ways of God. If God wants you to have wisdom and understanding in certain circumstances, His Holy Spirit will give you the words to say. God gives you the ability to heal the sick by the laying on of hands, cast out evil spirits who are in people in the Name of Jesus, speak in tongues, and to prophesy.

Once home after Bible Study, I prayed to God. I ventured into deep waters and broke my faith boundary, I asked God to bless me with His gift of Holy Spirit and to speak in tongues. I had to override my doubting thoughts and Satan's lies that were telling me that I was not doing it correctly. I spoke in tongues! Practice makes perfect. At first, my speaking in tongues language was small. As God matured me over time, my speaking in tongues gift, ability, and language has greatly improved. I can speak in tongues and He speaks to me more! I just have to be obedient.

People sometimes say to me, "Oh, you must have a hard life." I do not think I do. I am not a special case because I go through trials as well as victories just like any other person. Our intimacy levels with our Lord may be different, but it is our choice to walk as close to Him as we want. Sure, my pace is slow so it takes me triple amount of time to complete tasks, such as getting ready for the day, eating, folding laundry, and using the computer. Please do not pity me! My Cerebral Palsy, nonverbal, drooling, gag or coughing reflexes, and my left side of my body is more pronounced to my Cerebral Palsy than my right side of my body is all I know.

I live life to the fullest because I am a beloved daughter and child of God. I am God's treasured possession, and transforming in Jesus Christ's image! My life has meaning as God has revealed. My desire is to follow Him wholeheartedly and be a vessel to let Him glorify Himself in everything!

My Bible verse for my life is John 9:3 which states, "Neither this man nor his parents sinned," said Jesus, "but this happened so that the works of God might be displayed in him." I have had many believers who assumed that I wanted to be healed from my disability and quoted Scripture verses of Jesus healing people. I have had people who prayed over me because I was not confident enough to say, "No, thank you." Sure I face daily challenges more than other people and that does not bother me because my aim is on seeking God, knowing Him, and helping others know Him intimately. I do not understand the reasons behind life's circumstances unfolding. I can step out in faith to know that God will do what He wants. Time is becoming shorter until the day that Jesus comes back on the earth. As a child of God, I need to be spreading the gospel. No one else can spread or act like Christ as I can. Others may not stand up for Jesus. God created me unique! I have a purpose that God made for me and only I can fulfill it. So I need to believe, study, obey and follow the Holy Spirit to do God's will. I need to act how I want to be judged by Jesus! My intimate relationship with God Almighty has molded me to be content in being physically disabled and nonverbal. God has a plan and I just have to follow Him!

Now that God has blessed me with the Holy Spirit living in me, I smile and wave to people in hopes of them seeing Jesus Christ. I am beyond blessed to have Jesus Christ's light shining in me and to have His joy in my heart as I continue to seek Him wholeheartedly! I want to love people like Jesus. I want to pray with people, lend a helping hand, and encourage them by telling them about God and His gospel. God has taught me that the best way to spread His gospel to people is by living His gospel out actively; not being ashamed!

God has helped me to be created and transformed in His image. I am a new creation! My going through the motions lifestyle and addictions have been forgiven as well as erased. I do not know what God has in store for my life, but I am eager to experience the seasons! I am on fire for Him and my anchor holds within the veil! A spirit written life can be a messed up life transformed into a beautiful life filled with God's everlasting love, hope, joy, and peace when God is first priority in it!

About The Author

At the age of eight, Emily developed a desire to become an author to communicate with people. As God matured Emily in life, Emily read many books written by various authors who wrote about their experiences living with disabilities.

Emily had to be willing to be molded into Jesus Christ's image before His plan and her desire came to completion! After being turned down by seven publishing companies and at the age of twenty-five years old, God blessed Emily with an open door of possibilities for being a published author!

God has chosen Emily to write books. He's fulfilling her dream and desire to impact His kingdom! With the help of God's Holy Spirit, Emily has published Open H†S Word, Chap†er By Chap†er, and Dimly Lit as well!

CPSIA information can be obtained
at www.ICGtesting.com
Printed in the USA
JSHW030307060223
37307JS00003B/77

9 781948 237574